Chapters:

1. **Understanding Price Action and Price Momentum**
   a. Price action from open to close
   b. Stocks that go higher usually go higher
   c. Stocks that go lower usually go lower
2. **Why Options Greeks Do NOT Matter**
   a. Explaining the Greeks
   b. Soft deltas vs. deltas
   c. FAR
3. **Win Rate is Not Important**
   a. Shooting a half court shot
   b. Probability, math, odds
4. **Psychology of Trading**
   a. Why do 90% of traders lose money?
   b. Go for a walk, get a workout in
5. **Understanding Historical Data and Backtesting**
   a. Does it work
   b. Does it make sense
6. **Why Options Are the Wave of The Future**
   a. ROI returns
   b. Speculation, hedge, volatility
   c. Stocks are manipulated
   d. Dark Pools in the Stock Market
7. **Trading Options for Beginner, Intermediate and Expert Traders**

Chapter 1: Understanding Price Action and Price Momentum

In a simple economics class, students will learn what a supply vs. demand curve is. I was very fortunate to learn this when I was at the age of 12. My father, who is one of the most intelligent people I have ever met, taught me this. He was not only intelligent in the sense of book smarts, but he had great street smarts. He was president of his class at University of Wisconsin-Madison, managed 20 plus lawyers at Ameritech as co-general counsel, but most importantly he understood people. He told me many times that he was not the smartest person, but he understands how people work, what motivates them, and how to get the most out of them. For this I am very grateful and I will always be in debt to him.

Let's go back to the lesson that he taught me on the supply vs. demand curve and how it works. It shows us that the value of anything in this world is the difference of what one person is willing to pay for the product and what another is willing to sell it for. The point in the middle is where the acquisitions or trades happen and we will go over many examples to help illustrate this point a little bit better.

In our first example we will look at bottled water. This bottled water probably costs less than 7 cents to produce. This is not the point. The point is how much I am willing to pay for this bottled water. If I go to the grocery store and I am used to paying $4.99 for a case of bottled water and today they are charging $10, then I will not buy it. I then jump in my BMW and go out on a hot summer day in San Diego and that am thirsty and I see a guy standing at the corner selling bottled water for $1 each. This is the exact same bottled water that I could buy at the store for $.25, but I am thirsty so I will pay $1 for this same item, but not much more than this. That night I go to the Padres game and have a few beers. All I want is a bottle of water so I am hydrated and more importantly not hung-over. I can buy that same bottle of water that I bought at the store for $.25, on the street for $1, for $5 inside the stadium. If I want water there I have no choice but to pay. This is just one example of how price can change based on supply and demand.

We will now explore our second example and this is a common one that I give at all my webinars. I own a house in Chicago (I actually do) and I want to put it on the market to sell. I get the comparable sales in the area and then decide to list my house for $500,000 since I think that that is the fair market value. There are five bids for the house that come in but the highest bid is $450,000. The house sits on the market for 9 months with nobody willing to pay my asking price. Well, I think the market has now told me how much my house is worth and it is not worth $500,000 it is worth way less than that.

Let's say the opposite happens and I get higher bids than my offer. There are two bids at $500,000, one bid at $525,000 and one bid at $550,000. Well now that the market has told me that my house is worth more than $500,000, it is worth something in between $525,000-$550,000 if not more.

These are perfect examples showing us that anything in the world is worth the difference between what a buyer is willing to pay and the seller is willing to take. We will talk more about how this concept of supply and demand actually applies to the trading world.

I gave two examples of how the supply vs. demand curve works in housing and bottled water market, but the first time I learned about this is when I was only twelve years old.

My father was always a fan of hobbies: coaching me in basketball, baseball, soccer but more importantly trading and collecting comic books and baseball cards. This was fascinating to me because I could make money of a product made of paper or cardboard just because it had a picture of Michael Jordan on it. I am sure most of you remember the Beckett pricing guide this was one of the best things I had ever seen. This told us how much a baseball card, basketball card, or football card was worth. The thing about this was it only came out once a month. Can you imagine trading stocks every single day and knowing what the price was only once a month?

This created great opportunity for me to trade these baseball cards, comics, and most importantly football cards as I learned about supply vs. demand. It was a fact both fans and speculators collected cards of players they thought were going to be great. The better the player was, the higher the price of their card. Fans would love to collect cards in many different ways: the complete set, individual cards, or even their home team. Beckett gave the pricing for all these cards, but it only came out once a month. So, let's say a player got hot in between the releases of the guide their card would go up in value. We would then have to ask ourselves how much the card would go up in value. Just like the example of the house, it was the difference of what one was willing to pay for it and another would be willing to sell it for. How did I take advantage of this?

In the Beckett guide all the main players would have a value and everyone else would be known as "commons." There are two types of people at baseball card and comic book shows. There are the people that attend that are fans and there are the people that owned tables, who tried to take advantage of this supply vs. demand curve. These shows were open to the dealers an hour before the public. So, I would study all the box scores and games and look for opportunities to buy underpriced "common" cards of players who had good games that week. Before the show was open, I would go around and try to buy these "commons" or hot players from dealers that were not watching the games as much as me.

I remember Byron "Bam" Morris got hot and I would buy his football rookie card for $.10. I would then go back to our table and sell them all to fans. Every time I would sell them the price would go higher. This is because of a simple supply vs. demand curve. The fewer cards I had left the more they were worth. The more people that wanted to buy them the more they were worth. With baseball cards, stocks, options, futures or forex if there are more aggressive buyers than sellers than the price goes higher, and if there are more aggressive sellers than buyers the price goes lower.

You can apply this to anything in the world: baseball cards, comic books, cars, a house, but most importantly in the US stock market.

How much is a stock worth? That is the question that we are going to explore and I will help guide you through the value lessons of supply vs. demand and understanding how stocks work.

Let me start by talking about my opinion of the US stock market. It is a fact that the majority of stock market participants are long stocks and the US stock market in one form or another. Hedge funds, mutual funds, IRA, pension funds, individual 401k's, and individual investors are all LONG stocks and the stock market. We have all learned what happens when there are more aggressive buyers than sellers in any asset. Simple and easy, the price goes higher. So in theory the US stock market and stocks will ALWAYS go up in the long run, because there are more buyers than sellers. However, as a trader this long term time frame is less important to me. I am trading to profit on the moves in the market in the short term.

Every single day when the US stock market opens it is a battle between the bulls and bears in individual stocks and the broader market. In the long run there are P/E's, growth rates, revenues, and a number of other fundamental indicators at play but in the short term none of that matters. So our goal is to figure out if stocks are going higher or lower. How can we determine this? The answer to this is price action and price momentum. Lets first look at a candlestick. This tells us four important pieces of information.

A simple candlestick shows us the open, close, high and low during a certain period of time. On the daily chart if there is a red candle that means that the stock moved lower from open to close. If there is a green candle the stock closed higher from open to close. This is very important because this shows us price action and price momentum. I want to buy stocks as they go higher and sell them as they move lower. I do not want to go into too more depth about this topic right now, I just want to talk about how I trade this.

I look at six main stocks on the 5 minute bar:
AAPL, BABA, FB, GPRO, TSLA and TWTR.

Chapter 2: Why Options Greeks Do NOT Matter

When a person decides that they want to start trading for the first time they have many different products that they can choose between. A person can trade futures, forex, stocks, or equity options. There are many different advantages and disadvantages of trading each of these products, but in my opinion equity options are the best product to trade. We will look at why I think this is the case, but for argument sake let's just say that you also decide to trade equity options.

I have lost money in a day, a week, a month and I even lost about $140,000 in 2009. Can you imagine showing up to work every single day and not getting paid, but also paying someone else to be there. It is a terrible feeling and hopefully not one I will go through again. With that being said, I am proud to say that I have made millions in profits from trading options. I have not had a losing year in 6 years, but more importantly I am proud of the education that my team and I provide on a daily and weekly basis.

I am proud to tell everyone that I run a 10-man team and three of my moderators of my trading room were former students. They used to pay me money to listen to me trade, but now they are paid to share their knowledge, opinions, and trading styles with others. Throughout the 3.5 years that I have been in the education space, we had over 1000 FREE webinars, sold about 10,000 educational courses, and taught around 50,000 students how trade options better. In this book, I try to bring the best ideas together to make you become a better trader.

One of the most overrated aspects of trading is looking at risk through the Greeks, but before we can explore this we need to go over what each of the Greeks are.

There are two separate definitions of delta:
Definition #1: The amount an option will increase or decrease in value with a one-dollar move in stock price.
Definition #2: The percentage chance that the option expires "in the money" on expiration.

Example: AAPL is Trading $120
The Weekly 115 Calls have an 80 delta and are trading at $5.60
The Weekly 120 Calls have a 50 delta and are trading at $2.00

The Weekly 125 Calls have a 20 delta and are trading at $0.50

Once again, the delta shows us how much the option should move in price and the percentage chance of the option expiring "in the money" at expiration. We can say that the weekly 115 Calls will have an eighty percent chance of expiring in the money and a twenty percent chance of expiring worthless. The 120 Calls will have a fifty percent chance of expiring in the money and a fifty percent chance of expiring worthless. The 125 Calls will have a twenty percent chance of expiring in the money and an eighty percent chance of expiring out of the money. Note that in the money calls will have a higher delta the closer they are to expiration because there is a better chance that they expire "in the money." The out of the money calls will have a lower delta the closer they are to expiration because there is a lower worse chance that they expire in the money.

We also have said that the delta shows the dollar amount that the option will move with one dollar of underlying stock movement. If AAPL moves up 50 cents in value the options will move up .50 times their delta. Lets explore this a little better. If AAPL moves from $120 to

$121 how much will all of these options be worth?

Example: AAPL moves from $120 to $121
The Weekly 115 Calls will move $0.80 higher from $5.50 = $6.30
The Weekly 120 Calls will move $.50 higher from $2.00 = $2.50
The Weekly 125 Calls will move $0.20 higher from $0.50= $.70

If we wanted to look at which option gave us the best ROI we could look at that as well.

The Weekly 115 Calls return was $.80 divided by $5.60= 16% Returns
The Weekly 120 Calls return was $.50 divided by $2.00= 20% Returns
The Weekly 125 Calls return was $.20 divided by $.50= 40% Returns

In general, if a stock makes a "FAR": Fast Aggressive move in the Right Direction the out of the money options will always give us a better return on investment.

As AAPL moves from $120 to $121, we know that the chance of the 120 Calls expiring in the money this week will move higher. So the delta must move as the stock moves. This is a very confusing concept, but this is where **Gamma** comes into the mix so let's explore this.

Gamma is the amount the delta moves with one dollar of stock movement.

If AAPL moves from $120 to $121 and the $120 Weekly Calls move from a 50 delta to a 60 delta with one dollar of stock movement then we know that the gamma must be 10. If the AAPL $115 Weekly Calls move from a 80 delta to a 85 delta with one dollar of stock movement, then we know that the AAPL $115 Weekly Calls have a 5 Gamma. As AAPL moves from $120 to $121 and the $125 Weekly Calls move from a 20 delta to a 25 delta, then we know that the gamma for those is 5.

Gamma sounds tricky and confusing, but just remember it is the amount the "delta" moves with one dollar of stock movement.

AK Tip and Trick: The gamma will always be highest at the money and closest to expiration. Weekly options always have huge gamma, huge theta, high risk and high reward.

Lets re-explore the pricing of options with the Gamma component.

Example: AAPL is Trading $120
The Weekly 115 Calls will have an 80 delta, 5 gamma and are trading at $5.60
The Weekly 120 Calls will have a 50 delta, 10 gamma and are trading at $2.00
The Weekly 125 Calls will have roughly a 20 delta, 5 gamma and are trading at $.50

Now if AAPL moves from $120 to $121 with the gamma involved, lets look at how the options pricing will move with delta and gamma

The Weekly 115 Calls will move $5.60 plus $.80 plus $.05= $6.45
The Weekly 120 Calls will move $2.00 plus $.50 plus $.10= $2.60
The Weekly 125 Calls will move $.50 plus $.20 plus $.05= $.75

Lets go back and revisit the ROI of these options:

The Weekly 115 Calls return was $.85 divided by $5.60= 16% Returns
The Weekly 120 Calls return was $.60 divided by $2.00= 30% Returns
The Weekly 125 Calls return was $.25 divided by $.50= 50% Returns

This is a general rule of how much an option "should move" with one dollar of stock movement, but we have yet to explore some very important concepts like Theta and Vega.

Options can be used for two reasons speculation or protection. We can compare options to an insurance policy. Think of your car insurance. If you pay $1200 a year for your car insurance you could break that down and say that you pay $100 a month. If you wanted to break it down even further, you pay $3.33 per day for car insurance. Break it down even further into 24 hours in a day and you could now say that you pay $.17 per hour for your car insurance. If you are out of town for a weekend and do not drive your car for 8 hours. You do not get a refund for the time you didn't drive. This is very similar to the way options work.

Many big firms such as Goldman Sachs, Barclays, and Merrill Lynch use options as protection against their positions. As a general rule everyone is long the stock market through 401k's, IRA's, mutual funds, and pension funds. In a simple supply vs. demand curve, if there are more buyers in the market than sellers the price goes higher. If I am long an asset how would I go about protecting that asset? I would use options.

We have talked about how car insurance works and why it costs money every single day a trader must understand that the time decay is not linear in options. Let's look at an example to better illustrate this "time decay" concept which is described with the greek Theta.

Let's say that Facebook, FB, is trading $80 and the July 81 Calls are trading $2.00 and there are 20 DTE left. (DTE means days until expiration) A trader might say to themselves, "If there are 20 DTE and the out of the money option is trading $2.00, then the option must go down in value about $.10 a day"

During days the stock market is slow a trader will want to avoid buying premium or options because seasoned traders know that options will decay in value. As a former market marker I had two choices to make to avoid time decay

1. Lower the implied volatility of an option, thus making it cheaper and me avoiding that option.
2. Moving the date of my option forward thus decreasing the value as well. If you watch very carefully you will notice that the price of an option will decrease in value around noon and often times faster on a Friday. As I have said

time decay is NOT linear and the option will not decrease in value the same everyday and many options will hold much value until the week of expiration.

The last Greek that we must look at is Vega. This shows us how much an option goes up or down in value with a one point move in implied volatility. As a general rule implied volatility is the hardest concept for new traders to understand. There are two types of volatility; implied and historical. Historical volatility shows us how much a stock has moved over a given period of time. Traders at the CBOE would always look at the historical volatility over twenty days. This represented roughly one month of data for the stock. Then we would look at the implied volatility and this is where it can get tricky.

Implied volatility represents how much the market is implying the stock can move in the future. I often say that you can use the past to predict the future, but it does not mean it will always happen. We can use the historical volatility as a base for expectations. However this does not take into consideration uncertainty which can come in the forms of earnings, drugs announcements, and mergers and acquisitions. All of which affect the price of options.

There is always a good question that is asked at interviews for trading jobs, so let me give it to you and see if you can get it right.

XYZ is trading at $100 and it is currently July 18th 2015. The August 100 Straddle is trading at $10. Two weeks go by and the stock does not move at all. Does the price of the straddle go up or down in value? Most of you would say that the price of the straddle goes down in value since time has gone by. What if I told you that it is possible the price of the straddle went up in value? How is that possible? What if the straddle decayed in value $2.00, but the implied volatility went from 20 to 200 because the stock had a pending drug announcement expected to happen in September, but it is now happening in 3 weeks.

The beginning of this chapter started by talking about how the Greeks do not matter as much as everyone thinks they do. In order to understand the most accurate price of an option we must take into consideration all of the Greeks. I

Delta is the easiest Greek for most people to understand so we will start there. Most traders buy out of the money options, because they hear stories how calls or puts go up in value 500-5000% overnight. This is very true, but this is very often times for the "land of the hopes and dreams." This can happen, but if a trader always bought calls or puts waiting for this to happen they will blow out their account.

Is it possible for the price of a call to decrease in value if the stock moves up? Most of you might say of course it isn't. Lets look at an example from GOOGL from Earnings. GOOGL was trading $540 and the weekly 550 Calls were trading $5.00. Let's say that this is the price of the option the Thursday night and GOOGL report earnings the next morning and these options expire on Friday's close.

If we bought the GOOGL weekly 550 calls for $5.00, then we would need GOOGL to be trading at $555 just to breakeven on the trade. So, in theory GOOGL moves up in value to $554 and expires there then the 550 calls would be worth $4.00 and with the stock moving up in value $14, the calls actually decreased in value by $1.00. How can I make money buying calls? Well what if GOOGL goes to 640 dollars then lets explore the ROI of stock versus the options.

If GOOGL moves up in value from $540 to $640 and a trader was long stock then there profit would look like the following: $100/$540= 18% Gains

However, if a trader is long the GOOGL $550 weekly calls, if the stock moved up in value from $540 to $640, then these same calls would be worth $90 at parity the next day.

Let's look at the ROI on this trade now: $90/$5= 1600% Gains

We can see that calls are great to trade if a stock makes what I call "FAR" Fast Aggressive Move in the Right Direction. If the move to the upside does not happen fast enough or aggressively enough the calls could fall in value. Let's explore another strategy and this one often gets newer traders into trouble.

Yes it is true that a call that is $.20 has a better chance to double in value than a call that is $5.00, but if we get that slow climb higher, then the in-the-money calls will often move up value, but the out of the money Calls could decrease in value if the move is not fast enough. Let's look at a similar example from a trade I did in BP.

BP was trading $41.20 and a trader bought the July 43 Calls for $.24

I had a couple of choices of which option I wanted to buy for myself. Let's look at the two options I could have purchased. I could have bought the:

July 39 Calls for $2.50 with a 80 delta, and a gamma of 5 OR
July 43 Calls for $.25 with a 20 delta and a gamma of 8

Four days later, BP went up in value to $41.50 and both of these options moved, but they moved in opposite directions:

The July 39 Calls went to $2.70 increasing in value by $0.20 or about 8%, but the July 43 Calls went down in value to $.20.

What I am trying to teach you, that you will never learn in any other book or webinar is it is possible for calls to decrease in value as the stock moves higher because the implied volatility is moving lower and time decay is coming out of that option. As I have stated and I will continue to state, greeks are important if you want to look at the big picture, but reward and risk is far more important.

We are going to look at one more example of how theta and implied volatility affect options prices. From our earlier example, if XYZ August 100 Straddle was $10 and the stock did not move for an extended period of time is it possible for the straddle to increase in value? The answer is yes, because the implied volatility can increase in value causing options premiums to increase as well.

Let's look at a position in GE:

GE position:
Long 5,000 Deltas
Short 6,000 Gammas
Long 1,300 Theta
Short 6,000 Vega

Looking at this position I would notice a couple of things:
1. I want the short to go higher because I am long deltas
2. I want the stock to not move too much because I am short gamma which also usually means short premium
3. I am long theta which means that every single day that goes by and the stock does NOT move I make money via time decay.

4. I am short implied volatility so my position should make money in the event of a move lower in implied volatility.

The main thing that I want be aware of in this position is theta. Just because I am short theta does not mean my position will make money every day that GE is flat. It is possible for the implied volatility to increase in value more than the time decay erodes value so the options could actually increase in value. This was a position I often had on the trading floor in GE and I would look at it like this.

Many days, my P&L would not reflect the time decay, but it would eventually come in.

Once again, I am teaching you the things that you cannot read in books and it took me 12 years of the trading on the trading floor to learn these things. Greeks are so important, but it is much more important to understand the risk and reward set-up.

Chapter 3: Win Rate is Not Important

    a. Shooting a half-court shot
    b. Probability, math, odds

I have traded professionally for over 14 years, and let me tell you there has been some good days, good weeks, months, and even years but I would never tell you that I make money every single day, week, month or even year. In 2009, I lost over $140,000 in a year. Can you imagine going to a job, clocking in everyday to not only not receive a paycheck, but to actually pay to be there. This was one of the worst feelings I have ever had in my life.

I have often times tried to figure out how many options and shares of stock I have traded in my life. I have probably traded close to 50 million shares of stock and 5 million equity options all on my own account with the P&L going straight to my pocket. I traded on the floor of the CBOE from 2002 to 2012 and this was one of the best times in my life. The first day I came to the trading floor I was so nervous because I read Michael Lewis' Liar's Poker and thought that every trader was a drug addict, loved alcohol, and would gamble on everything. I could write a book about the crazy things I saw on the floor, but those men and women working in the pits were amazing traders.

My career started when Bota Capital Management hired me under their clerk to trader program out of the University of Illinois at Champaign-Urbana. They were willing to pay me $2,000 a month but more importantly they teach me how to trade the hardest product in the world, equity options. Traders in New York trade stocks and futures and few of them understand how complex options can be. So as a 22 year old this was my chance to prove myself in the world to my parents, friends, and most importantly myself.

I was never a great student, and often struggled to take school seriously. In high school, I graduated in the top 20% at a very good public high school and in college I graduated from the business school with a 3.4 GPA. None of those things are going to impress anyone, but the trading job gave me my chance to prove myself. If you ever meet me in person, you will realize that I am critical of everyone in this world, but I am most critical on myself. I know that I can do anything in this world that I want to do. I approached my first trading job with this mindset studying every single piece of options knowledge I could and learned as much as I could clerking for some of the best traders in the world. They taught me one of the most important things I have ever learned

"The true test of a champion is not how well he does when he is on top, but how well he does when he is down and out."

Michael Jordan said it best "I've missed more than 9000 shots in my career. I've lost almost 300 games. 26 times, I've been trusted to take the game winning shot and missed. I've failed over and over and over again in my life. And that is why I succeed." When I watched the Bota traders trade I noticed not only how well they dealt with gains but with losses as well. I talk a lot that trading is so very similar to playing poker. The best poker players in the world always end up with all the money, but they could lose in a day, week, month and even a year. Trading is the same way. Successful traders don't make money every day, but when they do lose money they pick themselves up and get back in the game.

Trading is not something everyone is equipped for. Just like I know I could never play in the NBA. It does not matter if I practiced basketball for 10 hours a day I simply do not have the athletic ability to do it. It is the same thing in trading, but what most people do not realize in trading is 90% of trading is actually emotional. It is how you deal with a losing day, week, month or even year. I will always remember a couple of things in my trading career. I will always remember the day I lost $180,000 in CECO, which is the worst losing day I have ever had. Then I remember the day I made close to $484,000 in AAPL. Then there was the 16-week, $30,000 a week losing streak in AMAG. These are things that I will always remember. However I have been profitable 13 of the last 14 years trading. The point of the story is that the win rate does not matter, the end P&L matters.

I will not name names, there are some really good mentors in the trading world but there are also some really bad ones. There are 3 simple questions a trader should ask their mentor:
1. Do you trade with real money? Most of them are going to answer yes.
2. How often do you trade?
3. Can I see a real P&L statements?

If a mentor cannot provide these, then run for the hills. Also be wary of someone's quoted "win rate." Someone could have a win rate of 90% but that does not necessarily mean they are a profitable trader. It is easy to set up a strategy with a high win rate but this generally leads to a unfavorable reward to risk setup and a chance of a large loss.

I go to the gym with my buddy and he says, "I'll bet you $100 I could make a full-court shot." I laugh and take the bet, knowing there is not a good chance he makes that shot. What if he wants 100-1 odds on it? The chance I win is still very high but the amount I have to risk makes this bet unfavorable now.

Know we can think about this in terms of trading. An options delta is the percentage chance that an option expires in the money on expiration. If someone gave me $5 million and said "AK I want 95% of all my trades to be winners" I could easily set up a strategy to do this using options deltas. I would sell a $1.00 Call Spread for $.01 (with a 1 delta) knowing that I would make money 99 out of 100 times, but that does not mean I will be profitable in the long run. Let's look at the example below.

1. I take a trade where I risk $500 to make $1000 and I will be profitable 40% of the time.
2. I take a trade where I risk $5000 to make $100 and I will be profitable 50% of the time

If we looked at the two examples, the bottom example will be profitable a higher percentage of the time, but I will be risking more money. Bottom line, it does NOT matter the percentage of trades that are winners. Let's look at one more example before we move to the next chapter

I take 4 trades, the first 3 trades I lose $1,000 per trade and then on trade #4 I make $5,000. So the breakdown would be 1 winner, 3 losers. Only 25% of my trades were winners, but I was net profitable $2,000. Ill take that any day of the week and that is why I am a profitable trader over time, because I understand risk vs. reward set-ups.

Chapter 4: Psychology of Trading

90% of all traders lose money trading and the average lifespan of a retail trading account is only 18 months. Why is this? It has to do with the risk vs. reward setups that retail traders take and how those returns work in longevity.

When you go to Las Vegas everyone knows that the house always has the advantage right? Have you ever gone to Las Vegas and won money? If the house has the advantage how can a normal player playing by the casino's rules actually make money? In the short term, anyone in trading or in Las Vegas can make money, but in the long term unless you are playing with probability on your side you are doomed.

What does that have to do with trading at all? Well, it has everything to do with trading, this is the way the average trader looks at their trading account. Most people take their bonus, extra money they have made and try to make money trading. I am here to teach you through this book that this is NOT how a person should think.

One of the main aspects of success in trading is having an understanding of probability and math. If I can take a trade that has a 60%

chance of winning how often would I take that trade? I would take that trade every single time, because I know in the long run I will make money just like the Las Vegas casinos. The Las Vegas casinos will always end up on top because the math and probability is in their favor. Let's look at another example to talk about the reason that so many traders lose money trading. Let's look at poker.

I used to play a lot of poker in Chicago and I would play Texas hold 'em and Omaha. Let's look at Texas hold 'em. I always say that I am an above average poker player better than most but not better than the best. When I am playing poker I might get into a couple of hands with the good players at the table, but instead of trying to outplay them I usually just aim for the weaker players at the table. When I am playing now I try to focus all my energy and effort on playing against those weaker players. I know that if I continue to play against them then I will have a better chance of winning in the long run. Let's also talk about a couple of hands of poker.

If you have played any Texas hold 'em before, you should know that pocket aces is the best hand to get. Winning with that hand feels good, but it often feels that you did not earn it. I know personally it is a much better feeling winning a hand with a small pair and calling out another player's bluff. Many trader want to make "hero calls" like this but it is not a good approach to trading.

Many traders want to call the bottom in JCP at $9 and try to short GOOGL at $700 and they are trading against the trend which as we have established is very difficult to do. I was introduced to the Ichimoku Cloud in 2006 when I took a break from trading for 5 weeks and I was hooked at that very moment. The reason that the Ichimoku Cloud works so well is because it makes a trader trade with the trend. Once I learned about the Ichimoku Cloud it was only available on a couple of major charting packages, but as the popularity has grown it has been adopted and picked up by almost all major online brokers. I don't want to go into too much detail about it I just want to focus on the fact that it keeps a trader on the side of the trend.

Chapter 5: Understanding historical data and backtesting

There are so many mentors in the business that teach options and stock trading and don't get me wrong there are a lot of very good educators. However there are also a lot of very bad educators. I was taught how to trade by some of the best traders in the world. My former colleagues at Botta Capital Management stack up against almost any trader out there. I try never to talk poorly about my peers, but I just would be very skeptical of some of the mentors there are.

I have watched so many webinars on trading. I have made money trading in my trading career, but I have also lost money in my trading career. I am proud to say that made money in 11 of my 13 years trading and my total profits are close to $5.5 Million. That doesn't mean as a trader that I haven't gone a day, week, month, or even a year without losing money.

So, when you are watching a webinar and there is a mentor or trader talking about trading, I would ask him three very simple questions:
1. Do you trade a real dollar account?
2. How often do you trade?

3. Can I see your statements from a broker that shows your P&L.

Let's explore these a little bit more in depth before I talk about back testing strategies, because I think that this is a topic that is so important.

Question #1: Do you trade a real dollar account? Everyone I mean everyone is going to yes to this question. Some mentors teach, but they can't make any money at all trading. Why would you ever want to learn from someone who isn't willing to put their money where their mouth is? The reason that I trade a real dollar account is because I believe that my trading will be profitable. I preach what I believe in and I am willing to put my money where my mouth is. Most traders in a webinar will say, "of course I trade real money." You have no idea how big their position is and to be honest they do not have to disclose it. Just because a mentor that is giving a webinar is trading a real dollar account does not mean that you can trust them at all. Then we go to question number 2.

How often do you trade? I have been in this business for a very long time and there is NEVER a best time of the day to trade or best day of the week to trade. Anyone who tells you otherwise has no idea how to trade. When I was on the trading floor, I would try never to ever leave. I risked getting $500 fines for eating on the floor, just so I would not have to leave. Yes it is true that there is the most action on the opening and closing bell, but that doesn't mean that there isn't money to be made in the middle parts of the trading day. Some of my best trading days happened on holidays or in the middle of the lunch break. I was the youngest trader in the GE pit for a long time, and "the older guys" would go and take lunch for an hour. I would love this because it gave me opportunity.

A broker would walk into the trading pit with a 5,000-lot order of options. Lets say 10 guys showed their size, amount they were willing to trade, of 1,000 each. If they traded everyone would get 500 lot even though they showed 1,000 options because the business would have to be broken up into 10 guys. If there are less people there then the traders would get their quantity, or 1000 each. Other traders in the trading pit were competition against you so the less traders in the trading pit the better. I would always try to stay on the floor all day and used to love when the "older guys" would go get lunch because if there was a good trade that happened that meant more money in my pocket.

Yes it is true that there are more orders at the beginning of the day, but you never know when a great order will come in. There are people in the business that try to convince others that there is only money to be made on Mondays or at the opening bell but the fact of the matter is that this is not true and a great trader is always in front of the computer screen trying to make money. If I miss a trade that I could have made $200 or $300 during the day I get mad at myself. Moral of the story, don't trust a trader that isn't trading at all times of the trading day.

The final question is about a mentors P&L. My clearing firm was Goldman Sachs and I used to get printed statements from them every single day and not once did I get a statement that was an excel document. Anyone can make up an excel document where it shows them being profitable. If someone giving a webinar shows you a excel P&L statements or does not show you a P&L statement run for the hills. As I am writing this book in 2015, my P&L statement is down for the year and I am not afraid to show it. This is the first time in 6 years that I have lost money trading, but it happens. This is the rollercoaster of a trading so if you think you have what it takes you must have a strong stomach.

The next point I want to make is on backtesting.

I like to compare trading to sports so let's look at it like this. If I told you the Chicago Cubs were 3-0 on Monday afternoon games when they started a left handed pitcher and the other team had a player with the last name of Smith, is this strong enough of a signal to bet on the game? The answer is no. Yes it is true that the Chicago Cubs are undefeated on Monday afternoon games when they start a left-handed pitcher and the other team has a player with the last name of Smith. However this does not show a meaningful relationship.

How about if I told you that AAPL goes up every Monday when it is down on Friday in the month of October, but the date has to be an even date not an odd date. Would this be an actionable trading idea? The answer is no. There are too many variables.

What if I told you that 8 of the last 10 times AAPL had earnings the stock rallied from the close of the day before earnings to the next day. Is this an actionable trading idea. The answer to this is yes, it makes sense, AAPL has low expectations on earnings and the stock moves higher because it has a good quarter. Let's know take these concepts and move them to the idea of back testing.

In back testing, we should always ask ourselves these questions:
1. Does the strategy make money in the past?
2. Does why it is profitable make sense?

As we talked about there is historical volatility and implied volatility. The historical volatility shows us how much a stock has moved over a given period of time and the implied volatility shows us how much the market makers are implying the stock can move in the future. The historical volatility helps us imply the future, but can never predict the future. Just like a relationship, we can use the past to help to predict the future, but we never know what the future will bring. Past performance is not indicative of future results. However backtesting can help gives us some useful insights, as long as we know what we are looking at.

Let's talk about the game of Craps. Once a number is hit, a player can make money if any number is rolled with two dice except for 7.

The house wins with 7 and you might ask yourself why this is. It is because a 7 will show up with two dice more than any other number and that is why it is the houses' number.

Simple and easy, if you are trading based on historical results say to yourself: 1. Does it make money? And 2. Does it make sense that it is making money?

Chapter 6: Why Options Are the Wave of the Future

Stock trading is dead, let me repeat myself again, stock trading is dead. I am very fortunate that I was around when there were trading firms that would hire a young eager college grad. When I was graduating college in 2001 from the University of Illinois Champaign-Urbana I has no clue what I wanted to do with my life. I had a finance major and a concentration in accounting, but I really had no clue. I graduated with as little effort as possible with a 3.4 GPA which was good but not great. I crushed every business class I took and got a C+ on every "easy" class such as Astronomy, Classic Civilization, etc. I knew that I was not a 9-5 sit in a cubicle kind of guy. I asked the person that I respect more than anyone in the world, my father. "Dad, what should I do with my life." He then told me that I should be a trader.

He took me downtown to lunch and I remember seeing the "traders" wearing yellow colored jackets and all they did was act like fools and yell and scream at each other. I didn't want to be one of those guys. I had interviews to be a financial advisor, financial analyst, and investment banker but I loved the questions that I was asked at my trading interview.

Questions such as how many windows are there in New York City? Probability and math questions. I decided to give it a go and went to the clerk to trade program at Botta Capital Management. We started with 14 guys and only 4 of us made it through the program and were given the chance to trade equity options for a living.

There are many products that a trader can trade: stocks, futures, forex, and equity options. Equity options are hands down the hardest to trade because there are so many variables that determine their value such as: delta, gamma, vega, theta, and rho. I mean stocks are easy, if you are long it and it goes up you make money, if you are short it and it goes down you make money and it doesn't move at all you are flat.

What about if I told you that you could risk $100 to make $900 if a stock don't move at all. In equity options trading there a strategies that I will teach you called Iron Butterflies, Iron Condors, Call Butterflies, Put Calendars and many others.

I was very lucky that I was taught how to trade by some of the best traders that I have ever seen and I was taught the product that is the wave of the future, equity options. Stocks are boring and don't move much in the day, 1% at most, they require huge amounts of margin and capital to trade. Equity options now come into the picture. There are options that I have had positions on that have moved from $.50 to $28.00 for and winners for 5000% returns when the stock has only moved 25%. This is the reason the options are the wave of the future. Let's explore this a little bit more in depth.

ROI stands for Return on Investment. Currently the 10-year interest rate pays a whopping 2.25%. That means that if you invest in it you get paid $225 on a $10,000 investment per year, sounds boring. Equity options are a way to play a stock, speculatively where a trader can make 100% gains in hours or 5000% returns in weeks. This sounds too good to be true, but with all the potential upside there is a downside.

There are many times that I have purchased an option for $1.00 and watched that option move all the way to zero. With all the good there is bad. However with proper risk management and a trading plan options are the best way to trade any stock and where you think the stock is going. I tell traders all the time that you cannot trade unless you have an opinion. Your opinion is not always right but you have to have an opinion to trade. Why do institutions trade options?

It is true that options are very complex and hard to understand, but lets break it down very very easily. There are two types of options. There are calls and there are puts. A call option gives the owner of the option the right but not obligation to buy 100 shares of stock at a certain price (strike price) at a certain date (expiration). A put option gives the owner of the option the right but not obligation to sell 100 shares of stock at a certain price (strike price) at a certain date (expiration).

Why would someone want this right? Let's say that Facebook (FB) is trading $100 and I thought it could go $120 on earnings but I do not want to risk too much money. I could buy 100 shares of stock for $100 which would cost me $10,000 and then if the stock went up to $120 on earnings I would profit 20% or $2,000. However if I buy the Facebook March 110 Calls for $2.00 it would only cost me $200 and if Facebook went up to $120 then these Calls would move up in value from $2.00 to $10.00 good for 500% returns.

Options give us a better way to speculate, but they can also be used as a hedge against a stock position. When institutions are buying calls they are either buying calls as speculation to the upside or they are buying calls as a hedge against a short stock position. When I watch institutional order flow I never know if a trader is buying it for speculation or a hedge.

Puts are bought for one two reasons as well, a hedge against a long stock position or speculation to the downside. Using my trading plan will help to put the math and probability in my corner. Institutions take million dollar bets in the options market but that does not mean they are right.

Andrew Ross Sorkin did a report about a year ago and said that about 25% of all mergers and acquisition stocks had unusual options activity in their names and am I not surprised by this. I had a stock about a year and half ago that was a Chinese insurance company ticker PL. On Friday an institution bought a couple thousand Sep 70 Calls for $1.10. I saw this order and bought 30 of them for $1.10 or $3300 of risk. Over the weekend they announced the company was going to be purchased for $80 cash and these calls went from $1.10 to $10.00 and my

30 lot or $3300 of risk netted me close to $27,000 in profits.

Did the SEC or OCC go after the trader that profited $1.8 Million over the weekend on this deal? Maybe, I'll probably never know. All the information and trades I see come from a scanner which shows publicly traded orders so if a trader is trading on insider information and I make the same trade as them it is possible that that trader can go to jail for insider information, but I can not.

One of the most interesting books that I have read in the last couple of years is Flash Boys by Michael Lewis where he talks about dark pools and algo trading. Dark pools get such a bad rap in the industry as hidden order centers where traders place orders that the public cannot see. To be completely honest, the dark pools were created to upset the algo traders, which I believe is a great thing for the industry. For those who don't know what a Dark Pool is it can be easily explained. A dark pool is a center of off exchange liquidity where traders can transact without their volume or price action reported to the trading public. This makes it nearly impossible to make money day trading stocks.

I tell anyone who will listen that day trading stocks is hands down the hardest thing to do and making money in the long run is now even harder. Equity options do not currently have dark pools and the exchanges are fighting very hard never to have any dark pools. So, this is just another reason why trading options are the wave of the future, the ability to see every single institutional order from all the big hedge funds and hedge fund players.

Chapter 7: Trading Options for Beginner, Intermediate and Expert Traders

I am a very large trader and trade a huge quantity of stocks and options during the day. This was not something that happened overnight for me. When I first started to trade I was a very small trader and only traded a couple of different equity options names like GE, KRFT, and PEP. GE was my bread and butter and moneymaker. I started with Botta Capital management making $3,000 a month plus a "discretionary" bonus. This means that it did not matter how much money I made trading, they would decide how much of that I would get to keep. I started trading 20 and 50 lots and later in my career I would trade up to 1,000 lots. A thousand lots controlled the right but not obligation to buy or sell 100,000 shares of stock. However, I started small and worked my way higher. Let's talk about this.

Everyone wants to jump in and start making money right off the bat, but that is NOT the proper way. Let me give you a little quiz and see if you can get it right, what do Brett Farve, Tom Brady, and Aaron Rodgers all have in common? If you were sports nut like myself you would say that is easy they are all starting QB's and have won Super Bowls, and the answer is correct. However what you did not realize is that they all started on the bench for more than a year until they got their chance. That is what every trader should be doing. Not jumping in head first without knowing if there is any water in the pool.

Let's look at one more example of this: Michael Jordan.

Michael Jordan is arguably the best basketball player ever. He won the Rookie of the Year, he averaged over 38 points a game in his second season, but it took him over 6 years to win a NBA championship. Why? He had some skills, but he then found Phil Jackson as his coach and mentor to get him to the next level. I want to be everyone's coach and mentor. Almost everything that you have done trading I have done myself. I lost over $490,000 in AMAG and to this day, I have no idea what the company even does. You would think that that money was in one day; no it was paper cuts of about $30,000 a week for 16 weeks. Let me be there to teach, guide, and take you to what you want to be: a professional trader.

Starting right off the bat there is so much information out there, so many mentors, newsletters, and traders to listen to. I am not going to sit here and say I am the best but I have a style and people seem to like it and that probably explains why we sold products to close to 3,000 different traders last year. Find someone you like to stick to them.

First, decide a product that you enjoy trading. I say that every single trader is different and they have different risk tolerances, style, feel, and approaches. You can trade futures, forex, stock or my favorite equity options. They all have their own advantages and disadvantages that I will help you guide through.

Futures are a great product and you can trade them 23.25 hours a day, but there are algos out there that know how to "run the stops." I think futures trading in oil, gold, and S&P are great for swing trading but often times can be challenging and frustrating for day traders.

Forex is the BEST product for a beginner trader to learn how to trade. There is a famous quote, "if you make a bad trade based on the chart, then you read the chart the wrong way." A trader can start trading forex with as little as a couple of hundred dollars. I like to trade them on the 4 hour bar using the Ichimoku Cloud. The disadvantages of forex is I could be in a trade for 4 weeks and not have a target hit or stopped out, once again a little too slow for me.

Then there are stocks. So many traders love to trade stocks because they are easy, if the stock goes higher, which they usually do over time, then the trader makes money. I say that day trading stocks is 100% the hardest thing to make money on. Also, throw in the fact that are high in commissions and margin makes them one of the WORST products to trade. Then we have my bread and butter: equity options.

In my opinion equity options are 100% the best product to trade. The reason is because a trader can double, triple even get 1000% gains within a few hours, days or even weeks. However with all the benefits there are disadvantages like implied volatility and time decay. When I am trading if I like a position or trade often times I will average down and buy an option at a cheaper price point. Sometimes that works well, but sometimes it doesn't. For example if I buy 200 call options for $.40 and in two weeks and the stock has sold off and the option goes to $.30, I will add to my position and buy more of them. This is a very expert move and I would not suggest it for a beginner or intermediate trader, but it often works out well for me. I don't mind adding to the position if it is losing money because I know that I still have time left on the trade and that options can only go to zero. We need to explore the roles of a beginner, intermediate and expert trader before we can move forward.

A beginner trader is anyone who is just learning to trade and is not making money or is losing money. 90% of all traders lose money and the average trader lifespan is between 1 month and 1.5 years. I say that there is NO shame with trading in a simulated account before trading real money. You can trade just as if it was real money but it isn't. If a trader cannot make money in this account they probably should find a better career.

Traders should have a daily loss limit as the most amount of money they are willing to lose in a day before they turn their computer off. I think daily loss limits should be about 5% of your account, so if you have a $10,000 account and lose more than $500 in a day, its time to turn the machine off. I have a confidence plan that I use in my trading so traders know my confidence about my individual trades. You can get it here for free:

As I talk about a beginner is a trader who is new to the game and is NOT making money. I have structured my trading differently since I left the trading floor. When I was on the trading floor as the biggest individual market maker in the world in AAPL from 2006-2009, I traded mostly implied volatility with a little bit of directional plays. I would trade every strategy from Call Calendars, Jelly Rolls, and Reversal/Conversions. Now I mostly trade calls and puts outright and it is much easier in my opinion to make money this way.

I have created a stop loss and exit plan for beginner, intermediate and expert traders for options and I want to share it with you. A beginner trader should use a 20% stop loss with 4 or 5 exits on a trade.

Let's explore this as a trade.

A beginner trader buys 40 Facebook Jan 120 Calls for $1.00
In theory this would be $4,000 of risk. This is TOO much for a beginner trader so I suggest using a 20% stop loss or $.20. I could put a stop loss in at $.80. As long as the stock doesn't gap lower overnight we have now cut our risk from $4,000 to only $800 on this trade. Now for exits. I like to use a very easy plan and you can always adjust it however you would like.

Exits: Sell 25% of the position or 10 at $1.10
(10% Profit)
Exits: Sell 25% of the position or 10 at $1.20
(20% Profit)
Exits: Sell 25% of the position or 10 at $1.35
(35% Profit)
Exits: Sell 25% of the position or 10 at $1.50
(50% Profit)

This would net on average sale of 40 units at
$1.31ish. So on this trade we risked $800 and
we netted a profit of $1200ish (40 * .31).
Overall a great trade. A beginner trader can also
move their stop loss to breakeven once Target
#2 is hit. This then GUARANTEES profit on the
trade. Let's look at this.

Exits: Sell 25% of the position or 10 at $1.10
(10% Profit)
Exits: Sell 25% of the position or 10 at $1.20
(20% Profit)
MOVE Stop from $.80 to $1.00 on the 20 left
Exits: Sell 25% of the position or 10 at $1.35
(35% Profit)
Exits: Sell 25% of the position or 10 at $1.50
(50% Profit)

Now you have a great equity options trading
plan for a beginner. Lets move on to an
intermediate trader.

I describe an intermediate trader as one that is either making money or has moved their profitability from negative to positive, but is still not at the level they want to be at. Yes, they are making money but not enough to quit their job, trade full time, or support themselves on just the money they are making trading.

An intermediate trader should use a 50% stop loss with 4 or 5 exits on a trade. Let's explore this as a trade.

A beginner trader buys 100 Apple March 130 Calls for $.50
In theory this would be $5,000 of risk. This is TOO much for an intermediate trader so I suggest using a 50% stop loss or $.25. I could put a stop loss in at $.25. As long as the stock doesn't gap lower overnight we have now cut our risk from $5,000 to only $2500 on this trade.

I like to use a very easy plan and you can always adjust it however you would like.

Exits: Sell 25% of the position or 25 at $.60 (20% Profit)
Exits: Sell 25% of the position or 25 at $.70 (40% Profit)

Exits: Sell 25% of the position or 25 at $.85 (70% Profit)
Exits: Sell 25% of the position or 25 at $1.00 (100% Profit)

This would net an average of around $.31 in profits. So on this trade we risked $2500 and we netted a profit of $3100ish (100 * .31). Overall a great trade.

Again, a trader can move their stop loss to breakeven once Target #2 is hit. This then GUARANTEES profit on the trade. Let's look at this.

Exits: Sell 25% of the position or 25 at $.60 (20% Profit)
Exits: Sell 25% of the position or 25 at $.70 (40% Profit)
MOVE Stop from $.80 to $1.00 on the 20 left
Exits: Sell 25% of the position or 25 at $.85 (70% Profit)
Exits: Sell 25% of the position or 25 at $1.00 (100% Profit)
MOVE Stop from $.80 to $1.00 on the 20 left

Perfect, simple and easy: now you have a great equity options trading plan for an intermediate trader.

I am not sure if you smart traders noticed but the profit percentages on example number 2 were much different than example number 1. I prefer to trade lower priced options and I am not talking about $.05 or $.10 options, but options that have a 25 to 35 delta around $.50-$.80 because I can get a much better ROI on them. Let's look at this example before we move forward and they will explain why cheaper options have a better chance of returning a better ROI.

XYZ is trading $30 and I have two choices:
1. I can buy the XYZ Jan 27.5 Calls for $3.50 (Delta: 80)
2. I can but the XYZ Jan 32.5 Calls for $.50 (Delta: 20)

If XYZ opens up $2 higher tomorrow, the XYZ Jan 27.5 Calls will move roughly to $5.10 or about 40% profits while the XYZ Jan 32.5 Calls will move $.90 or 80% profits. This is why I prefer out of the money options to trade using Unusual Options Activity. Let's move to an expert trader.

An expert trader is one who has been trading for at least 3 years and always makes money. Yes they can have a bad day, week, month or even year but they make enough money to support themselves. This is where I am at in my trading career and this is where I want everyone to get to. Once the last 4 years I have came up with 14 on demand courses and DVD's, three books, taught 50,000 plus students and the reason for that is to "pay it forward." I have been fortunate to make millions trading so I want to give back to others.

In my opinion an expert trader is one that does NOT have to use stops and I do NOT use stops in options. What I do is exit a position if there is not much time left in the trade, my feelings about the stock or stock market has changed, or technically the chart looks weak. I have no problem adding to a losing position. This has helped me out of some bad jams, but also hurt me as well.

Experts are experts, just like a poker player. The best poker players in the world do not make money every day, week or even month, but they feel when they have the best hand, when the other player is bluffing and when they have the right probability and math in their corner. Trading is the same way. Wherever you in your trading career I want to get you to the next level. It is going to be a bumpy ride and it will not be all lollipops, bicycle rides, and picnics, but believe and trust in me.

Chapter 8: Different Types of Risk

I was at home and night and I noticed the Nikkei was down like 2% and I thought that is oversold, so I went to my account and bought a 1-lot future not having any idea how much risk that even was. I had about $100,000 in my trading account at that time. I left to play with my dog and then noticed that my P&L said I was down $24,000. I freaked out, because the market did not move much, but the fact was I was trading a product that I did not know the risk. I then called James Ramelli, my right hand man and asked him about it. I was freaking out and he then explained it was in Yen terms so it was only about $60. The mortal of the story is no matter what the product is, make sure that you always understand your risk in what you are trading.

For futures, oil is a BEAST it is $1,000 a 1 lot in a $1 move, that's some big boy trading when S&P 500 Futures Minis are only $50 per 1 point move. For more information on risk and margin requirements, please visit: www.cme.com

Stocks also have HUGE risk even if you put stop losses in them because they can gap overnight. Stocks are only open from 6am until 8 pm central. There have been many times when a stock has gapped overnight up or down and no stop loss can protect you from that. So understand that stocks can be risky as well even with the proper stop losses in place. I want to move back to my bread and butter: equity options.

There are so many factors that involve in the option market. We know these are time decay, delta, gamma, implied volatility, dividends, and interest rate risk. I want to explore something a little bit more. I tell all my subscribers that anyone can trade weekly options or earnings, but understanding risk is very important. A trade that has $500 in risk in the weekly options is MUCH more risky than a trade that has $500 of risk and has 6 months left. As traders we have to understand our risk and I want dig into this a little bit more.

I trade three main strategies: Earnings, the Ichimoku Cloud, and Unusual Options Activity.

I have a cardinal rule that I will almost always sell all of my options I am long the day before any stock has earnings. Unusual Options Activity works great but I think it is more of a crapshoot for earnings so this is a rule that I have adopted. If I want to take a trade for earnings it will be a spread and I will have less risk on this trade. That is one general rule for risk. Let's explore the other main one:

On the trading floor, we had something called "DTE," which meant days until expiration. That tells me how many days are left until the option expires. We all know that weekly options have the highest gamma, theta, and also represents the highest risk and highest reward. After that the front month options represent the next highest risk and reward and chronologically through the expirations. We need to realize this risk.

AAPL is trading $115 and does NOT have earnings

I buy 50 AAPL Weekly 120 Calls for $.20 (Delta: 20, Gamma: 10, Theta: 5) ($1000 of Risk)
I buy 10 AAPL Front Month 120 Calls for $1.00 (Delta: 25, Gamma: 5, Theta: 2) ($1000 of Risk)
I buy 2 AAPL Jan Leaps 120 Calls for $5.00 (Delta: 30, Gamma: 1, Theta: 0)

Let's say that AAPL opens up the next day up $1 and the implied volatility on ALL these options remain the same. What is the profitability of these options?

50 AAPL Weekly 120 Calls for $.20: Delta plus Gamma minus Theta:
These Options have gone from $.20 to $.45 and $1250 Profits

10 AAPL Front Month 120 Calls for $1.00 Delta plus Gamma minus Theta:
These Options have gone from $1.00 to $1.28 and $280 Profits
2 AAPL Jan Leaps 120 Calls for $5.00 Delta plus Gamma minus Theta:
These Options have gone from $5.00 to $5.31 and $62 Profits

This shows us that the weekly options will give us the highest reward on our money but they also will have the highest risk. We talked about DTE and we should look and what if AAPL does NOT move at all overnight.

50 AAPL Weekly 120 Calls for $.20 will lose $.05 or $250.
10 AAPL Front Month 120 Calls for $1.00 will lose $.02 or $20 total
2 AAPL Jan Leaps 120 Calls for $5.00 will not move at all

With the positives there are always going to be negatives. Trading weekly options and trading earnings are fine for any trader, but understanding the risk involved is so important and this is why I put together a little guide that can help you with your risk:

With $100,000 in my account I am willing to risk:

The Risk Parameters are equal (roughly)
Weekly Options: $500 of Risk
Option with 2 Weeks left: $1000 of Risk
Option with 3 Weeks left: $1250 of Risk
Option with 4 Weeks left: $1500 of Risk
Second Month out Option: $3000 of Risk
Six Month Out Option: $5,000 of Risk

Chapter 9: Entries and Exits

There is an old expression, "it is very important for a plane to take off, but it is much more important for it to land." What does that mean? It is simple and easy. Putting on trades is the easy part and the difficult part is deciding when to book profits, let a trade ride, add to a position, or cut losses. This can be managed with a very easy and simple trading plan or maybe a journal.

When I was on the trading floor there was a firm that used to make all of their traders write down every single trade that they executed that day, why they put it on, was it profitable, and why they took it off. Trading is all about patterns and seeing if you can recognize patterns in yourself. Some traders trade well in the morning, because they get exhausted by the afternoon, some traders always have their initial entry as a long. So understanding how you trade and which stocks you trade well. It is so important if you truly want to become a professional trader yourself. I know personally that I trade very well in the morning because that is when the most action is and then it tapers down from there. I thrive in fast, volatile markets, when there are huge intraday swings.

I do not trade well in range bound markets and very slow bullish markets.

Another one of my friends used to tell me that in texas hold 'em, there is no such thing as a bad hand, just a bad flop. That means that you could be holding a 2 and a 7 in your hand, the worse hand in poker probability wise, but the flop could be 7, 7, 2. Wow, you just went from a very bad hand to a full house. I always say that as long as a trader has an exit spot, there is no such thing as a bad trade. I do think that probability and math will always triumph, but if a trader buys a bear bar after the stock has sold off from open to close 12 straight days, there is a chance that they could still make money on this trade. Let's explore this a little more and help you navigate through candlesticks and why they are so important when combined with the Ichimoku cloud.

A candlestick shows us price action and price momentum. A simple candlestick shows us four very important factors: the open, the high, the low, and the close. Candlesticks can be on any time frame and it is important to line up the proper product with how fast the product moves. A fast moving stock or commodity would be traded on a faster time frame and a stock or product that moves much slower would have to be moved to a longer time frame. When using the Ichimoku Cloud, these are the best settings for a trader to be trading on:

Forex: 4 hour bar
Futures: Day Trading, 12 minute bar, swing trading them: daily chart
Stocks: Daily bar unless day trading them then on a daily chart.

If a trader came up to me and said "AK I want 95% of my trades to be winners." I would say that is easy, but that does not mean that the trading account would make money. I know I could go out in the market and sell a $1.00 Call Spread for $.01 and that call spread would make money 99% of the time, but the one time it lost would eat up all the profits. Making sure that we have proper risk and reward set-ups is so important and when a trader is buying an option, time is always against them.

On the trading floor there was an old guy in my trading pit and his name was Paul. A broker would come into the trading pit and ask us for a market on an option. Let's say that based on our theoretical values we $5.00 bid at $5.20 100 up. This means that as a trader we would buy 100 at $5.00 and sell the same option at $5.20. This is how a market maker would make money in their career by buying on the bid and selling on the offer. Being a market maker is much different than trading as a retail trader because we are just trying to make money on the spread between the bid and offer on the options and on implied volatility.

If we bought the option every single trader would then try to go sell stock against their long calls as a "delta neutral" hedge against the position. If we got our hedge off then we would not often lose money on direction but we could lose money if implied volatility dropped.

Then there was Paul. The minute he bought those calls, he would offer them for $5.10. So, in theory if the stock moved higher Paul would lock in his $.10 profit. Most of the traders would be fine, because if you remember we sold stock against those calls. Paul though in theory was trying to make $1000 and willing to risk $50,000 (100 * 5.00 *100). This is obviously not a very good risk vs. reward set-up and the reason that Paul was no longer trading in the trading pits after a couple of months.

If anyone in the world told you that trading options is easy, they are wrong. There are so many variables and factors that play in mind. Understanding risk is one of the most important things when trading. Often times I compare myself to a hedge fund manager where I have to manage my risk. Often times I will sell positions not due to the fact that I do not like that trade, but do to the fact that I like another position better.

When I am trading, I watch Unusual Options Activity and things that I look at is volume, open interest, and the chart. I also look at the time that option has until expiration and understanding that $500 in risk in the weekly options is much more risk than $500 of risk in option position that is a year out.

I was recently in Nicaragua and I was told that it is a very dangerous country and they kidnap people for no reason very easily. So I took a cab from the airport to Puerto Cortes where my hotel was. The whole cab ride I was thinking of an exit plan. If the cab driver all of the sudden stopped on the side of the road, where would I run, do I have anything sharp in my pocket, what would I do. In trading it should be the exit same thing. Every single trader should have an exit plan of what to do in any trade. Is it a price of the option, price where the chart trade, time period during the day or will I hold it for a swing trade. All of these are so important. We all know that good traders think about how much money they can make but great traders know how much money they can lose if they are wrong. Simple and easy: never ever buy call options for $1.00 without a exit plan based on option price, stock price, or time period and that will greatly help your trading.

Made in the USA
Lexington, KY
28 July 2016